FANTASTICALLY
GREAT WOMEN
who made
HISTORY

kate Pankhurst

BLOOMSBURY

LONDON OXFORD NEW YORK NEW DELHI SYDNEY

JOSEPHINE BAKER

MARY WOLLSTONECRAFT

MARY SHELLEY

HATSHEPSUT

Sayyida al-Hurra

ADA LOVELACE

How did they become so fantastically amazing **and** great?!

To make history you need to be brave, bold and believe in yourself – just like the women in this book. They lived in times when women weren't expected to have big ideas, be in charge or to have exciting ambitions – but that didn't stop them. Their extraordinary deeds and words didn't just make history, they helped to shape the way we live today.

Read on and prepare to be inspired!

WANTED!
RUNAWAY SLAVE AND UNDERGROUND RAILROAD CONDUCTOR
HARRIET TUBMAN

BORN ARAMINTA ROSS, AROUND **1820** IN THE 'SLAVE STATE' OF MARYLAND, USA. CHANGED HER IDENTITY TO HARRIET TUBMAN WHEN SHE ESCAPED.

HAS SHAMELESSLY MADE REPEATED TRIPS TO MARYLAND BETWEEN **1850** AND **1860** TO HELP MANY MORE SLAVES RUN AWAY.

REPORT SIGHTINGS TO YOUR NEAREST SLAVE CATCHER.

You'll NEVER catch me!

Like many other African Americans in the south of the USA in the 1800s, Harriet Tubman and her family were slaves. This meant they were the property of a rich white household. To make money for themselves, owners forced slaves to work long hours, on land and in their homes, with no payment.

Harriet dreamed of a better life. After hearing stories of slaves escaping north, to 'free states' where slavery was outlawed, Harriet tried to persuade her family to run away with her. But they were too scared of being caught and punished. Even though Harriet was scared too, in **1849** she decided that freedom was worth the risk...

MARYLAND

FOLLOW THE TRACKS TO FREEDOM...

Runaway slaves, like Harriet, were helped to freedom by the **'UNDERGROUND RAILROAD'**. Although this sounds like a railway, it was actually a network of safe routes north. 'Underground' meant that it was top secret. It was set up by people, white and black, who wanted to put an end to slavery. They were called **'ABOLITIONISTS'**.

Travelling at night meant less chance of being caught.

If I follow the North Star I'll know I'm heading in the right direction.

SLAVE CATCHER

WANTED!

Harriet had to be careful to stay hidden from slave catchers.

REWARD

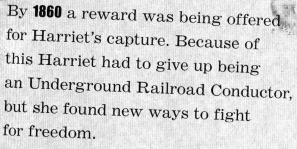

By **1860** a reward was being offered for Harriet's capture. Because of this Harriet had to give up being an Underground Railroad Conductor, but she found new ways to fight for freedom.

During the American Civil War Harriet served as a nurse and a spy, even leading a military expedition. Harriet's brave deeds helped to ensure that one day all slaves would be free – and at the end of the war, in **1863**, slavery was abolished.

In **1850** the **FUGITIVE SLAVE ACT** was introduced in order to make it harder for slaves to find freedom in the USA, even in 'free states'. But this didn't stop Harriet. She guided her passengers further – into Canada – to find safety.

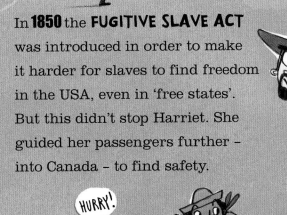

When Harriet reached the free state of Pennsylvania, she was, for the first time in her life, a free woman. But without her friends and family Harriet felt very lonely. She decided to use her freedom to help other slaves to freedom, and became an Underground Railroad Conductor.

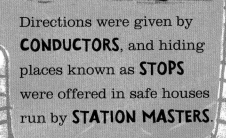

Directions were given by **CONDUCTORS**, and hiding places known as **STOPS** were offered in safe houses run by **STATION MASTERS**.

BOUDICCA

Boudicca was queen of the Celtic Iceni tribe during the Roman invasion of Britain in 43 AD. The Celts believed that women could be strong leaders, and with her fearless attitude, wild hair and brutal battle skills, Boudicca was a brave and powerful leader who inspired **TERROR** in all who met her. The Roman army made a **MIGHTY** mistake when, simply because she was a woman, they underestimated Boudicca.

FOLLOW THE SPEARS TO TRACK BOUDICCA'S BATTLE AGAINST ROME...

RAH!

When the rebels and the Roman army finally came face-to-face, Boudicca inspired her army to fight bravely, but, this time, they were defeated.

Boudicca's ferocious army took the Romans by suprise. Her uprising was threatening their hold on Britain.

Down with ROME!

Defeated but NEVER FORGOTTEN!

No one knows for sure what happened to Boudicca. Some think that, rather than be captured by the Romans, Boudicca poisoned herself. Other accounts say that she didn't survive the battle.

One thing is certain – mighty Boudicca wasn't afraid to defend her people and their way of life. That is why, 2,000 years later, her legend lives on.

We're in charge now!

In 59 AD Boudicca's husband died and she was left to rule alone. The Romans thought the idea of a female ruler was ridiculous and so told Boudicca they were in charge. Boudicca resisted and as a result she and her daughters were treated very cruelly. The Romans thought they had scared Boudicca off, but...

RARRRRRRRRRGH!

THEY COULDN'T HAVE BEEN MORE WRONG!

Watch out ROMANS!

Enraged by the injustice of what had happened to her and her people, Boudicca gathered a fearsome army of Iceni and Trinovante soldiers (a neighbouring tribe).

First Boudicca ordered them to attack the Roman town of Camulodunum. They showed no mercy, destroying a temple built in honour of the Roman Emperor and setting buildings alight.

CAMULODUNUM

Next they wreaked havoc on Londinium, the Roman town that later became London.

VERULAMIUM

Follow BOUDICCA!

LONDINIUM

The ROMANS will be sorry they messed with the CELTS!

Then, Boudicca marched on the Roman town of Verulamium, causing more chaos!

Flora Drummond

MARCH TOGETHER!

WE WILL GET THE VOTE

YES WE WILL!

go flora

follow FLORA!

COME ON GIRLS!

VOTES FOR WOMEN

Flora Drummond was born in Manchester, England, in **1878**, and grew up in Scotland. Flora wanted to become a post mistress but because of a rule which said that all post masters and mistresses must be at least five foot two inches tall, she was told she was too short to do the job. Flora was outraged – the rule didn't take into account that women are often shorter than men. Her height had nothing to do with how good she would have been at the job!

Standing tall, Flora decided to fight for fairer rights for working women, and in 1906 she joined the WSPU (Women's Social and Political Union). Women in the WSPU were called suffragettes. They fought for the law to be changed so that women had the right to vote and have a say in how the country was run.

THIS WAY SISTER SUFFRAGETTES! FOLLOW FLORA!

Flora's heroic attitude, enthusiasm and efficient organising skills played a huge part in leading women towards the equality they deserved. And in 1918, the right to vote was given to some women aged over 21.

I led my SUFFRAGETTE army to VICTORY!

Our voices will be heard!

go girls

We will not be IGNORED!

DEEDS NOT WORDS

CABINET MINISTERS SPECIALLY INVITED

Quickly Flora became a leading figure in the WSPU. She was known as 'The General' because she was so skilled at organising and inspiring her fellow suffragettes to do all they could to get...

VOTES FOR WOMEN!

The government tried its best to ignore the suffragette campaign but Flora made that very difficult for them to do indeed...

I wore military style clothing to lead my army of SUFFRAGETTES!

9th March 1906

SUFFRAGETTE IN 10 DOWNING STREET!

Oi!

Te he!

Security was breached at the home of Britain's Prime Minister by prominent suffragette Flora Drummond. While a fellow suffragette distracted police, Flora rushed inside before being promptly ejected. Her brazen intention was to hand out information about the Votes for Women campaign to the Prime Minister himself.

I am obliged to do nothing at all about women getting the vote. You can keep pestering though.

21st June 1908

THE GENERAL SETS SAIL FOR PARLIAMENT

There were shocking scenes on the River Thames today as Flora Drummond found another inventive method to force cabinet ministers to listen to the suffragette message. Unsuspecting ministers, who were enjoying tea on the riverside terrace of the Houses of Parliament, were unable to ignore Mrs Drummond's shouts as she sailed past on a barge, inviting them to join a suffragette march in London's Hyde Park!

I am inspired!

GET THE VOTE

Together We Are Strong

STAND TOGETHER

VOTES FOR WOMEN

TO VICTORY

FLORA is a STRONG leader.

5th October 1907

SUFFRAGETTES MARCH ON SCOTLAND!

A crowd of 10,000 cheering onlookers lined the streets to witness the spectacle of Scotland's first march in the name of women's rights. The procession was made up of around 1,000 suffragettes and was expertly organised and led by Scottish suffragette Flora Drummond.

Qiu Jin 秋瑾

Qiu Jin was born in China in **1875**. The way people lived in China had not changed for generations and this meant that, like most Chinese girls, Qiu Jin was forced to follow many outdated traditions.

One of the harshest of these traditions was foot binding – small feet were considered to be beautiful so young girls' feet were broken and tightly bound to make them as tiny as possible. This meant every step could be painful.

Most girls were not well educated but Qiu Jin was from a wealthy family and her parents allowed her to study the same subjects as her brothers. The more books Qiu Jin read, the more questions she had about the unfair way women were treated.

Wisdom gave Qiu Jin the words to stand up for change...

"BOUND FEET have always been a DISGRACE!"

Qiu Jin sometimes went by different names. Dushu Jijian meant 'read books, practise sword'.

Bound feet could be as small as 10 centimetres long.

"DO NOT tell me women are not the stuff of HEROES."

The Power of Words

At the time it was shocking for a woman to speak her mind. But Qiu Jin wrote powerful poems, passionate articles and gave captivating speeches about the struggles women faced. Shaking off the traditions that held her back, Qiu Jin unbound her feet and, in order to experience the same feeling of freedom men did, began to wear men's clothing.

The Power of Knowledge

In search of more inspiring wisdom Qiu Jin travelled to Japan to study where women were treated with more respect. Once there she joined people who believed that the only way to make China a fairer place to live was to get rid of the old-fashioned government that had ruled for centuries – the Qing Dynasty.

We must physically be fit to FIGHT for our RIGHTS.

"ARISE! ARISE! Chinese women ARISE!"

A Wise Warrior

Qiu Jin moved back to China where, in **1906,** she took a job as the head of a school. Her job was to secretly prepare students to rebel against the government. She led women in exercise classes (something very new) so they would be physically fit enough to fight.

Qiu used a traditional Chinese brush pen to write her poems.

Final Words of Wisdom

In **1907** Qiu Jin was warned that the government suspected she was involved in plotting against them. Qiu Jin knew that anybody caught plotting faced giving up their life, but she allowed herself to be captured. Wise and brave Qiu Jin wrote a final poem explaining that by sacrificing her life she was making the ultimate stand for what she believed in. These actions made her a hero in China and inspired other women to play an active role in the revolution of **1911**, which successfully forced out China's Qing Dynasty. Afterwards women were able to live more equal and fulfilled lives.

"Although I die I still live... Through sacrifice I have fulfilled my DUTY."

Qui Jin always found the right words and although her life was tragically cut short her wisdom lives on.

THIS WIRELESS RADIO BELONGS TO

NOOR INAYAT KHAN

UNLIKELY SECRET AGENT AND HEROINE OF WORLD WAR TWO.

MORSE CODE

A .-	G --.	M --	S ...	Y -.--
	H	N -.	T -	Z --..
		O ---	U ..-	
		P .--.	V ...-	
			W .--	

OCCUPATION: First female wireless operator to be sent into Nazi-occupied France during World War Two.

BACKGROUND: Noor's father was descended from Indian royalty and her mother was American. She grew up with a strong belief in fairness and tolerance of people's differences. This was precisely why, after being forced to flee the invading German army in her home in Paris, France, and go to Britain, Noor decided to join the WAAF (Women's Auxiliary Air Force) as a radio operator to support the British fight for freedom against the Nazis.

TOP SECRET MEMO FROM BRITAIN'S S.O.E. (SPECIAL OPERATIONS EXECUTIVE) MAY, 1943

Dear Noor,

You have proved yourself to be a skilled wireless radio operator for the WAAF and are fluent in French and English. We need people with skills like these to work as undercover agents, sending messages to a network of spies working for Britain in Paris. This network is known as Operation Prosper.

Your superiors tell us that before the war you worked as a children's book author. This makes you an unlikely candidate for the very different work of being a secret agent, but we have been told you are keen to offer your skills to help win the war. This is a very brave decision. If captured the German police, the Gestapo, will show no mercy.

Regards

S.O.E.

PS: Your codename is Madeleine. (The name is taken from a character in the book of traditional Indian children's stories you wrote.)

Agents hid their radio equipment in suitcases. This meant they could send messages from different locations and avoid detection. Coded messages were sent using Morse code, a series of dots and dashes.

MESSAGES FROM MADELEINE:

MAY 1943: London, do you receive me London? I have been in Paris for just 72 hours but have located radio equipment in the greenhouse of a fellow spy.

The Gestapo are EVERYWHERE!

The FASTEST response time OF ANY agent landing in the field.

July 1943: DISASTER! Operation Prosper has been compromised! Many agents have been arrested. I am the only radio operator left in Paris. Don't try and persuade me to return to Britain - I intend to do whatever it takes to keep communications open.

The average time a radio operator avoided capture was just SIX weeks. I managed to work in Paris for FIVE MONTHS!

September 1943: The Gestapo are desperate to catch me. I have to be very careful as they are driving around Paris with radio signal detection equipment hidden in bakery and laundry vans.

To evade capture I changed my appearance several times.

The Gestapo will never recognise me now!

SECRET CODES

TWENTY JATAKA TALES BY NOOR INAYAT KHAN

MISSION REPORT

Noor sent over **20** messages to London that helped to evacuate airmen who had been stranded in France, but in October **1943** the Gestapo tracked her down. Calling upon incredible inner strength Noor resisted arrest, made daring attempts to escape from prison and refused to give away any secrets.

Tragically, Noor did not survive being a prisoner of war. Her incredible efforts were acknowledged with the highest honour for bravery – the George Medal. Noor was one of the most remarkable agents of World War Two. Her work showed that in extreme situations ordinary people are capable of extraordinary things.

TRUST HER, SHE IS A DOCTOR!
DR ELIZABETH BLACKWELL
THE FIRST WOMAN EVER TO BE AWARDED A DEGREE IN MEDICINE

Elizabeth was born in England in **1821**, but grew up in the USA. Before the age of **24** Elizabeth had never considered studying medicine. Doctors discussed illness and the body, and these were thought to be highly unladylike things for a woman to study – but things changed when one of Elizabeth's friends became ill.

People found it extremely embarrassing to talk about their bodies, and Elizabeth's friend wished she could have been treated by a female doctor. She thought that Elizabeth, who was studious and hard working, would be an excellent doctor. At first Elizabeth couldn't imagine such a thing. But after more thought she realised that women deserved to feel more comfortable with who was treating them.

Just because there were no women doctors didn't mean there shouldn't be...

TRUST ME! I SHALL become a doctor!

knee

BRAIN

heart

ELIZABETH LEARNED MANY IMPORTANT LESSONS ON HER JOURNEY TO BECOMING A DOCTOR...

eye

DR Blackwell

Hand

BRAIN

foot

FIG 1: Elizabeth was rejected by **29** medical schools until, in **1847**, Geneva Medical College in New York State, USA, offered her a place.

FIG 2: When Elizabeth started at medical school she discovered that her fellow students had been asked to vote on whether a woman should join the course – they didn't think a woman would actually ever turn up and voted 'yes' as a joke.

FIG 3: Elizabeth studied hard. Her classmates and professors soon realised she was no joke. In **1849** Elizabeth became the first woman to be awarded a medical degree, graduating top of her class.

At first, nobody would give her a job, so Elizabeth travelled to Paris, France, to gain experience. Then, in 1857, Elizabeth opened a hospital where women were treated by female doctors – the New York Infirmary for Women and Children. She also taught at top medical schools and founded a medical college for women.

The pioneering work Elizabeth did made it easier for patients to talk about their bodies, paved the way for other women to be doctors and shaped the healthcare we receive today. Elizabeth showed everyone that women make very good doctors indeed!

POCA

THE CHIEF POWHATAN

VIRGINA

Pocahontas was born around **1595** and was the daughter of the chief of the Powhatan Native American tribe who lived on the eastern coast of what is now Virginia, USA. The way Pocahontas and her people lived changed forever when ships from Britain arrived in **1606**. The people aboard (known as colonists) called America the **New World**. They wanted to farm the land and set up towns (or colonies) even though the Native Americans already lived there and had their own way of doing things.

The two sides traded with each other, but there was also a lot of misunderstanding and conflict. Pocahontas, who was just a young girl at the time, tried to make the best of the situation by offering help and friendship...

Who are these strange new people?

LET'S CALL OUR NEW HOMELAND VIRGINIA!

I bring CORN and FISH.

JAMESTOWN

N
W   E
S

AND OUR COLONY JAMESTOWN.

HONTAS

1607: A colonist called John Smith was captured by Pocahontas's father. While being held prisoner Pocahontas taught him to speak the Algonquian language and he taught her to speak English.

I told a story that Pocahontas saved me from being killed by the chief. This story became very famous, but I was known for telling TALL tales so it may not be true.

This is a PEBBLE

The temporary PEACE my marriage brought was known as the POCAHONTAS PEACE.

1613: The relationship between the colonists and Native Americans got worse and even more fighting broke out. Because Pocahontas was the daughter of the chief she was captured!

If we hold Pocahontas hostage, the chief will have to release the colonists he captured!

Hold on! I was kind to you!

1614: While still being held captive Pocahontas married a colonist named John Rolfe. At the time women often had little say in who they married, so nobody can be sure exactly how Pocahontas felt about her new life. We do know that the marriage united both sides and brought peace (for a while at least).

Even though I dressed like a COLONIST on my journey to England I was still considered VERY different.

In **1616** Pocahontas made the long journey to England with her husband – she was one of the first Native Americans to go there. John Rolfe returned to England to raise money for the colony and to show others what life was like in Jamestown. The people Pocahontas met (including the king) wrongly thought Native Americans were wild and dangerous, but they quickly realised that Pocahontas was none of those things.

Even when she was far from home, in what must have been a very daunting situation, Pocahontas helped to grow the understanding that all people, no matter their culture, deserve respect and kindness.

REACH FOR THE STARS WITH
THE FIRST WOMAN IN SPACE

VALENTINA TERESHKOVA

Once you've been in space you appreciate how small and fragile the EARTH is.

BEEP BEEP.

BEEP.
BEEP.

CCCP

VOSTOK 6

One small but important detail was overlooked on Valentina's journey to space – a **toothbrush**! Valentina did have **toothpaste** though!

TOOTHPASTE

In **1961**, in the Soviet Union (now Russia), 24-year-old Valentina Tereshkova heard the amazing news that her country had sent the first man into space, cosmonaut Yuri Gagarin. (Soviet astronauts were called cosmonauts.) At the time the Soviet Union and the USA were competing to make breakthroughs in space exploration. The competition was known as the 'space race'.

The Soviets wanted their next 'space first' to be sending a woman into space. The adventure of space travel seemed a million miles away from Valentina's job in a textiles factory, until she discovered she shared a daring hobby with the first man in space – skydiving! If being able to parachute had helped Yuri Gagarin become a cosmonaut then maybe, just maybe, it might help her too.

In **1962**, impressed by Valentina's skydiving experience, the Soviet space programme selected her to train as a cosmonaut. Parachuting would turn out to be a VERY important skill. The only way for cosmonauts to make a safe landing was to parachute from their spacecraft as it fell back to Earth!

After more than a year of intensive training, in **June 1963**, Valentina's dreams soared higher than ever before. She was launched into space aboard the spacecraft *Vostok 6*...

THREE... TWO... ONE...
BLAST OFF!

Valentina's mission lasted **2 days, 22 hours** and **50 minutes** and made **48** orbits of the Earth.

Floating in zero gravity, Valentina monitored devices that tracked how space travel was affecting her body

and took photographs of the Earth's atmosphere.

MISSION (ALMOST) SUCCESSFUL

Everyone thought the mission was a complete success, but almost 30 years later it was revealed that Valentina narrowly averted disaster. While on her adventure, Valentina realised *Vostok 6* had been programmed to jet out into space on its return journey rather than safely back towards Earth! Valentina was asked to keep this mistake a secret so nothing would detract from her amazingly successful mission.

Valentina had ambitions that were out of this world

and dared to see how far her dreams could take her...

"I see the light HORIZON. A light blue. This is the land. How BEAUTIFUL it is! All goes well."

ADA LOVELACE

Follow Ada's story around the cogs...

Ada Lovelace was born in London, England, in 1815. She grew up during an age of invention, where amazing machines, driven by cogs and steam power, were created to do things faster and better than a person ever could. Ada had an incredible mind and like one of these great machines it *whirred* and *spun* with possibilities.

Numbers were one of Ada's great passions (her mother had studied maths and insisted Ada did the same). She also had an astounding imagination (Ada's father was a famous poet). Ada lived in a time when women were not expected to have ideas that could change the world. But she made an astonishing leap of imagination about technology and the future...

Wheeee!

From an early age Ada was intrigued by how machines worked. In **1828**, at just twelve, she designed a flying machine. She studied the wings of birds and suitable materials, and eventually designed a steam powered mechanical flying horse! (At the time the only way to leave the ground was in a hot air balloon.)

Ada put her ideas about flying machines in this book – 'Flyology'.

FLYOLOGY
BY ADA LOVELACE

FLYOLOGY

ink

In **1833** Ada became friends with mathematician Charles Babbage at a demonstration of his new invention the Difference Engine (a huge mechanical calculator).

Ada has a BRILLIANT mind.

It is as if thought itself has been mechanised.

In **1840** Charles revealed plans for a bigger, better calculating creation – the **Analytical Engine**. He didn't realise it at the time but he had just designed the beginnings of a modern-day computer. It would have been enormous, with thousands of moving brass parts, all powered by steam! Studying the thrilling invention, Ada's imagination whirred and spun until... **PING!** Her extraordinary mind went one step further than Charles's had. Ada realised that the Analytical Engine could do more than just make calculations...

If this machine can be instructed to process numbers it can also be instructed, or programmed, to carry out other tasks - like composing music!

Ada didn't know it, but she had predicted the age of computers. She even created a pattern, or 'algorithm', that could be read by the Analytical Engine – making her the world's first computer programmer, over a century before the first computer was even built! Sadly, Ada never saw her vision become a reality. Due to cost, the Analytical Engine was never built. But her contribution to computer science was a hundred years ahead of its time.

Sayyida al-Hurra

Sayyida came from a family of Muslim nobles who lived in the kingdom of Granada in Spain. In **1492**, when Sayyida was just a child, she and her family were forced to flee across the Mediterranean Sea to Morocco in North Africa. This was because Spanish rulers didn't want Muslim people living in their country. Sayyida never forgot the injustice that she and her family suffered, and it made her fierce and strong.

Aged 16, Sayyida married the Sultan of Tétouan (a city on the coast of Morocco). Tétouan was under threat of attack from Spain and Portugal. Queens did not usually have a say in military matters, but Sayyida seized her chance to fight back against the old enemies who had made her flee her home.

When her husband died, Sayyida continued to rule Tétouan. She was more determined than ever to drive Spain away from her shores and so decided to enlist the services of...

RUTHLESS PIRATES!

I will turn the tide agaisnt SPAIN!

PORTUGAL

SPAIN

GRANADA

TÉTOUAN

MOROCCO

AFRICA

One of the most fearsome pirates of the time was Barbarossa of Algiers. He and Sayyida were allies and between them they controlled the whole of the Mediterranean Sea, plundering treasure from Spanish and Portuguese ships. Sayyida also forced the Spanish and Portuguese to make deals with her by kidnapping important people from their ships and holding them for a ransom.

RABGGH!

Together we will RULE the SEAS!

The riches Sayyida claimed from Spain and Portugal helped Tétouan and its people to flourish. The city was rebuilt with docks for Sayyida's pirate ships, high walls to keep invaders out and winding streets to confuse intruders.

Don't expect me to give up being a pirate queen!

Eeeek! whatever you say!

Sayyida became so powerful that she set the terms for her next marriage, making the Moroccan sultan travel to her home in Tétouan to marry her. It was the first time this had happened in Moroccan history. After her marriage Sayyida remained in Tétouan, continuing to rule as the undisputed pirate queen for over **30** years.

THE WAVES SAYYIDA CREATED IN THE MEDITERRANEAN MEAN HER STORY WILL BE NEVER LOST AT SEA...

Sayyida al-Hurra is a title meaning queen. Sayyida's real name has been lost to history.

A WOMAN CAN BE KING!

HATSH

Hatshepsut lived **3,500** years ago in ancient Egypt, and was married to the pharaoh, Tuthmosis II. When Tuthmosis II died Hatshepsut's stepson was next in line for the throne – but he was just a baby.

Women couldn't be proper pharaohs so Hatshepsut took over as a stand-in co-ruler. She didn't have the authority of a pharaoh but could watch over Egypt until Tuthmosis III was old enough to become king.

THANKS!

I'll look after EGYPT for you!

Because Hatshepsut lived so long ago we can't be sure exactly what happened, but it seems Egypt faced a threat of some sort. Hatshepsut needed to show her people that a woman could be a strong leader in times of danger. She decided to give herself a new look, one that had worked for previous rulers... she ordered that all images and statues of her be made to look more masculine and king-like!

Head cloth and cobra worn by pharaohs

Broad shoulders

IF I act like a KING and look like a KING, I WILL be a KING!

Traditional fake beard worn by pharaohs

⋶PSⴎT

MAKING HISTORY

Hatshepsut DID become pharaoh – one of the most successful of ancient Egypt. After her **20**-year reign the now-grown-up Tuthmosis III became pharaoh of the peaceful and secure Egypt that Hatshepsut had built. One of her greatest achievements was the elaborate temple she had constructed and filled with enormous statues of herself as king. The solid stone figures and sphinxes represented how strong and powerful she was.

SPHINXES had a human head and the body of a lion. They were placed as guards outside temples.

LOOKING at these STATUES, nobody could question my POWER!

CHANGING HISTORY

Bizarrely, **20** years into Tuthmosis III's reign, almost all statues and images of Hatshepsut were deliberately destroyed! Hatshepsut had shown everybody that a woman could be pharaoh. But it is thought that this may have threatened the long tradition of pharaohs only being men, leading Tuthmosis III to take the drastic step of attempting to delete Hatshepsut from history!

Despite Tuthmosis III's efforts to erase all evidence of his stepmother, enough fragments of Hatshepsut's story have been pieced together for us to know that she was an extraordinary and very different sort of king!

HANG ON! You can't just chisel me away!

If nobody remembers Hatshepsut, nobody can question my POWER!

JOSEPHINE BAKE

"I improvised, _CRAZED_ by the music... Each time I _LEAPED_ I seemed to touch the sky!"

Josephine Baker was born in 1906 in St Louis, Missouri, USA. Her family were very poor and from a young age Josephine had to work to earn money.

When Josephine was growing up, black people were treated very unfairly. They weren't allowed to do the same things or go to the same places that white people could. This was called **segregation**.

To distract herself from life's problems, even just for a few moments, Josephine would do three things. Dance crazy new dances like the **Turkey Trot, The Itch**, and the **Mess Around**. Enjoy the thrill of laughter and applause. And pull funny faces!

At just 14 years old Josephine landed a job with a group of travelling musicians. Audiences loved her and at 16 she was given a leading role in one of the first shows with an all-black cast to be shown on Broadway (the famous theatre district of New York). Josephine was the talk of the town, but segregation meant that she would never be seen as an equal to white performers.

Josephine continued to wow audiences in the USA. One day she heard that there was no segregation in France. So in 1925, she took a job in a theatre in Paris...

R

Just like Josephine, Paris was dazzlingly different... oh la la...

Parisian audiences watched, mesmerised, as Josephine danced the Charleston (a popular dance of the time) like nobody had ever seen it before...

Bonjour Paris!

Whooo!

Fast footwork – c'est fantastique!

Yeah!

Come on!

There was fascinating face pulling – magnifique!

And extreme body bending – sacré bleu!

Josephine was a star! She became so famous that hair styling products were sold for women who wanted to copy her distinctive look! Paris was a place that Josephine could truly be herself – dazzling, funny and rather eccentric. (Josephine owned a pet cheetah called Chiquita, that became part of her Parisian act.)

BAKER OIL

TAH DAH!

PERFORMING TONIGHT! THE SENSATIONAL

JOSEPHINE BAKER

"Surely the day will come when colour means nothing more than the skin tone. When understanding breeds LOVE and BROTHERHOOD."

Josephine was so grateful to her adopted French home that during World War Two she put herself in danger by working as a spy for France.

Later in life Josephine adopted twelve children from around the world and used her fame to make a stand against racism. When visiting the USA she refused to perform in theatres that didn't allow black people to attend, and campaigned for an end to segregation.

Mother and daughter Mary Wollstonecraft and Mary Shelley both had a lot to say about what was wrong with the way people acted and treated each other. Their ideas were new and clever, but some people found them **SHOCKING** and downright **SCARY.**

Both women shared their ideas in books which are still read today, over two centuries later! Mary Shelley never knew her mother, as Mary Wollstonecraft died shortly after her daughter was born, but Mary Shelley was still hugely influenced by the ideas she read in her mother's books...

WOMEN should not be happy with their LOT!

MARY WOLLSTONECRAFT

In **1792** Mary Wollstonecraft was the first person to publish a book suggesting that women's rights should be the same as men's.

VINDICATION OF THE RIGHTS OF WOMAN

Vindication means showing that you are right about something. I was RIGHT that women are just as important as men.

She is a HYENA in petticoats!

The book **UNNERVED** many people. They were very used to the way things had always been and couldn't imagine a different way of doing things.

Say what you like. I know I'm right!

The loss of my mother drew me to books about EMOTIONS, I loved GOTHIC HORROR stories.

Gothic horror is a type of story filled with suspense and emotion.

In **1816**, when Mary Shelley was 18, a poet friend set a challenge she couldn't resist...

THE POET LORD BYRON

Write a story to awaken THRILLING HORROR!

I had heard of GRUESOME science experiments trying to re-animate dead bodies using electricity. ARGH!

A truly chilling story came to Mary in a nightmare. As her mother had done, Mary Shelley wanted her book to encourage people to think carefully about what was right and wrong. Frankenstein is a '**GOTHIC HORROR**' story about the dangers of not thinking through the consequences of your actions.

MARY SHELLEY

The great works of Mary Wollstonecraft and Mary Shelley inspired many people to think about the way we should live for the benefit of everyone.

RARRGH!

In the story, Victor Frankenstein brings a creature he built from human body parts to life. When the monster causes havoc, turning very nasty indeed, Victor is left wishing he had never created him.

ink

FANTASTICALLY GREAT WORDS

algorithm a pattern of mathematical steps or instructions

allies people who are on the same side as someone, for example fighting on the same side in a war

cabinet ministers the small group of people at the top of the British government

Celts a name for people who lived in Europe from around the 15th century BC to the 1st century AD

cosmonaut the name for an astronaut from the Soviet Union or Russia

evacuate get someone out of danger

fugitive someone who has run away

Gestapo the secret police force of Nazi Germany

Nazis the political group that ruled Germany from 1933 to 1945, including during World War Two

orbit a journey around something in space

pharaoh a king or ruler of ancient Egypt

plundering stealing

racism treating people differently based on the colour of their skin

rebel protest about or fight against laws or the people in charge

revolution a big change, such as when a government is overthrown or the political system of a country is changed

segregation keeping people separate – in the USA segregation laws kept black and white people apart

slave someone who is owned by another person and has to work in harsh conditions for no pay

Soviet Union a country that existed from 1922 to 1991, made up of Russia and many other states that are now separate countries

sultan a king or ruler of a Muslim country

suffragette a woman who campaigned for women to be allowed to vote

uprising when a group of people in a country start fighting against the government